WHATEVER HAPPENED TO AMELIA EARHART?

by
Melinda Blau

A
cpi
Book

From

RAINTREE CHILDRENS BOOKS
Milwaukee • Toronto • Melbourne • London

Library of Congress Number: 77-22173

Art and Photo credits

Cover photo and photos on pages 16, 29, 30, 35, 38, 40 and 41, Wide World Photos.
Photo on page 6, Henry Miller News Picture Service/New York Public Library
Picture Collection.
Photo on page 13, Paul Parker/New York Public Library Picture Collection.
Illustrations on pages 9, 18, 25 and 28, Connie Maltese.
Photos on pages 17 and 36, The Kansas State Historical Society.
Map on page 39, Alfred Fusco.
Photos on pages 33 and 47, Photo Trends.
All photo research for this book was provided by Roberta Guerette and Sherry Olan.
Every effort has been made to trace the ownership of all copyrighted material in this
book and to obtain permission for its use.

Library of Congress Cataloging in Publication Data

Blau, Melinda E   1943-
    Whatever happened to Amelia Earhart?

    SUMMARY: A biography of the woman who set many records as a pilot.
Discusses the mystery surrounding her disappearance while attempting to fly
around the world.
    1. Earhart, Amelia, 1898-1937—Juvenile literature.
[1. Earhart, Amelia, 1898-1937. 2. Air pilots] I. Title.
TL540.E3B58   629.13′092′4   [B] [92]   77-22173
ISBN 0-8172-1057-1 lib. bdg.

Manufactured in the United States of America.
ISBN 0-8172-1057-1

Contents

Chapter 1

Daredevil in Atchison

"I'll try it out first!" shouted seven-year old Amelia Earhart. With the help of her uncle and two cousins, Amelia and her younger sister, Muriel, had built their own roller coaster. The daring ride would begin at the top of their grandfather's toolshed.

Amelia climbed aboard the rickety cart that sat atop roller skates. But her first ride was a disaster. The little cart zoomed down and hurtled off the track. Its passenger flew forward and landed on the ground with a thud. Shaken but unhurt, Amelia insisted on trying again.

She was determined to make a successful ride on the homemade roller coaster. No one

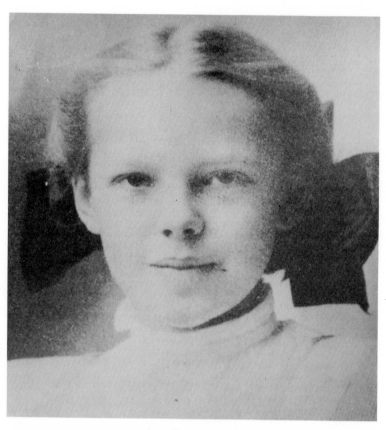

Amelia at seven.

knew then, not even Amelia, that she would become a world-famous adventurer. There was something else none of them could have known. *Amelia would someday be at the center of a mystery that would baffle the world for more than 40 years!*

Amelia Earhart was born in Atchison, Kansas in 1898. Her father, Edwin, was a lawyer for the railroad. His work often took him away from home. Amelia's mother, Amy, often traveled with him. This left the young Earhart girls with their grandparents much of the time.

Amelia's grandparents were shocked by her tomboy ways. Once, when Amelia jumped over the fence that surrounded their big house, her grandmother said, "When I was a small girl, I did nothing more tiring than roll my hoop in the public square!"

But Amelia's parents gave their daughters footballs, rifles, and boys' sleds. Mr. Earhart even took the girls on fishing trips.

While Amelia loved adventure, she loved books just as much. Only one thing bothered her: most of the stories were about or for boys. Amelia wanted to read about the great *women* of the world as well. That feeling stayed with her as she grew up.

Amelia was not like most young women of her day. She had great courage and non-stop curiosity. Whether it was testing a roller coaster, riding a horse, or zipping down a snow-covered hill, Amelia was always the daredevil.

Chapter **2**

Troubled Times

"Look dear! It flies," said a woman standing next to Amelia. The year was 1907, and the scene was the Des Moines State Fair. Amelia Earhart was seeing an airplane for the first time. Four years before, the Wright brothers had made their historic flight at Kitty Hawk.

The airplane Amelia was watching had two sets of wings, one above the other. The pilot sat in an open seat. He wore goggles over his eyes and placed his feet on a crossbar. An assistant stood on the ground near the plane. He spun the propeller. With that, the engine coughed and sputtered. First, the odd machine rolled along the ground. Then it rose into the air. Everyone below gasped at the sight. At least, almost everyone.

Amelia saw an airplane for the first time in 1907 at the Des Moines State Fair.

Amelia couldn't understand why everyone was making such a fuss. The strange-looking contraption looked like an ugly mass of rusty wire and wood. To nine-year old Amelia Earhart, the pony rides and merry-go-round were far more interesting than any airplane!

Amelia and her family had moved to Des Moines, Iowa a few months before. The move to

Des Moines was the beginning of unhappy times for the Earhart family. Mr. Earhart soon lost his job there. After their first year in Des Moines, the Earharts moved again. This time they went to St. Paul, Minnesota.

After the move to St. Paul, things went from bad to worse. Amelia's father was soon out of work again. The family picked up again, this time to Springfield, Missouri where Edwin had been promised a job. Instead of a steady job, he found only four weeks' work.

Edwin Earhart could no longer support his family. It was decided that they would split up. Edwin would go to Kansas City and try to open a law office. His wife and their daughters would live with a friend in Chicago.

Another move. Another school. Amelia had been like a rubber ball, bouncing from place to place since she had first come to Des Moines. But none of it could crush her spirit. She was determined to make something of her life.

In Chicago, Amelia decided that she wanted to get a good education in science. The bold seventeen-year old interviewed principals at several high schools. She also inspected their buildings. She refused the school nearest to her house because the chemistry lab was, as Amelia put it, "just like a kitchen sink."

During those years, Amelia thought of herself as a rather plain, homely girl. "I don't think that boys particularly cared for me," she later wrote, "but I can't remember being very sad about the situation." She had already decided, perhaps because of her own father's problems, that a woman should not have to depend on a man to support her.

Because of the constant changes in her life, it wasn't easy for Amelia to make friends. Her high school classmates called her "the girl in brown who walks alone." It was a description that would hurt anyone. But Amelia knew it hurt her most because it was true.

After her high school graduation, Amelia's family got together again in Kansas City. Her father was practicing law. But Amelia didn't stay home for long. She soon went to the Orgontz School, to prepare for college.

True to form, Amelia was an extremely ambitious student. As the headmistress of Orgontz put it, "Amelia was always pushing into unknown seas in her reading." But when it came to friends, she found herself on the outside once again. Most of the other girls were from wealthy families. They hadn't known the hardships that Amelia had endured. More important, her classmates were mainly concerned about getting married. Amelia wanted a career.

It was 1917, and the United States was involved in a bitter world war. Once, when she visited her sister in Toronto, Amelia visited base hospitals jammed with wounded soldiers. For the first time, she learned what war really meant. Amelia knew she had to do something. She wrote to her mother, "I can't bear the thought of going back to school and being so useless." After a quick Red Cross first aid course, Amelia took her place among the other nurse's aides at Spadina Military Hospital.

During that hard winter of 1917, Amelia found something that really excited her—*flying*. At a nearby military base she could watch the beginning pilots learn how to handle their planes. The more she watched these daring young men, the more she wanted to know about them. Amelia asked endless questions. What was it that made them fly? How did it feel to face *danger?*

During World War I, Amelia served as a Red Cross nurse's aide.

Amelia, of course, wanted to try flying a plane. But the men told her civilians were not allowed to fly—*and certainly not a woman!* Time after time, Amelia would return to her work at the hospital, angry with small-minded people. She promised herself that someday she would change that kind of thinking.

Chapter 3

Headspins and Tailspins

"Dad, please ask him how much it costs to learn how to fly."

Edwin Earhart couldn't believe that this was the same little girl who had once preferred merry-go-rounds to airplanes. But Amelia wasn't a little girl any more. Living with her parents, who had moved to California, she wondered what to do with her life.

A few days later, Amelia convinced her father to let her have "just one ride." The pilot was Frank Hawks, who would later become a famous racing pilot. He looked at the tall, thin girl in the high-laced shoes and thought to

14

himself—*another nervous female!* Hawks only agreed to take Amelia if she shared a seat with his friend. He wasn't taking any chances by going up with her alone.

Amelia didn't care. She would have done anything for that ride. Hawks took the plane up into the clouds. He leveled off at 2,000 feet. Now Hawks nosed his craft into a steep glide and tipped the wings to the right. As they turned, the wind whistled through the open cockpit and tickled Amelia's ears. She finally felt free and alive.

Amelia knew she had to learn how to fly. But lessons were expensive—about $1,000. Her father couldn't afford that. But nothing stopped Amelia. She took a job with the Los Angeles Telephone Company to earn money for lessons.

For her first instructor, Amelia chose a woman, Neta Snook. She thought a woman would be a more understanding teacher in this "men's world" of flying.

One of Amelia's prized purchases at that time was a leather flying jacket. It made her *feel* like a pilot, even though she hadn't yet learned how to fly. But Amelia didn't want to look out of place on the dusty flying fields in a brand new

Amelia (on the right) and Neta Snook, her flying instructor, standing next to the first plane she learned to fly.

jacket. So she slept in it for three nights! Then, to complete the picture, she snipped her hair short.

Finally, the big day arrived—*her first chance to fly alone.* Without fear, Amelia took the rickety plane up to 5,000 feet. She was good, and she knew it. Her landing was terrible, but that didn't matter. She had found her life. Amelia Earhart was not simply going to be the best woman pilot—she was going to be the *greatest flier of all.*

Amelia spent the next two years flying whenever she could. She wasn't earning enough at the telephone company to pay for her flying time, so she started driving a truck for a sand and gravel company. It was hardly a typical woman's job, but then there was nothing "typical" about Amelia.

Amelia made her first solo flight in this plane in 1921.

The Earharts were worried about Amelia getting hurt. There were lots of accidents in the early days of flying. And Amelia had a few "close calls." One time her plane crashed in a muddy field. The plane flipped over, leaving the young pilot hanging upside down in her safety belt! On another flight, Amelia's safety belt didn't work as well. Her plane crashed with such force that Amelia's belt broke loose and she went flying out

One of her "close calls" resulted in Amelia landing upside down in a field of mud.

of the plane. Amelia walked away from these, and other crashes, unhurt.

In the summer of 1922, just in time for Amelia's twenty-fourth birthday, her family had a wonderful surprise. They scraped together their life's savings to buy Amelia her first plane. It was a *Kinner Canary*, a small, yellow plane.

Six months later, Amelia asked her family to an air show. As they were sitting down, the Earharts heard an announcement: "Miss Amelia Earhart is going to try for a new woman's altitude record in her *Kinner Canary*."

As always, Amelia was determined. She took the small plane up into the clouds, higher and higher, through dense snow and fog. Suddenly, at 12,000 feet, she lost all sense of direction. "Was I flying one wing high? Was I turning? I couldn't be sure," she said later. "I tried to keep the plane in flying trim, with one wish growing stronger every moment—to see the friendly earth again."

At that point, Amelia decided to take a chance. It could have cost her life. She pulled the stick back and kicked the plane into a spin. She reasoned that the force of gravity would pull the plane down. Finally, at 3,000 feet, the fog broke.

She could see the ground again! Amelia zoomed out of the spin and landed the plane safely. One of the old-time pilots came running toward her as she stepped out of the plane.

"What were you trying to do?" he shouted. "Suppose there had been a fog all the way down to the ground? We would have had to dig you out in pieces!" Refusing to be alarmed, the calm young woman looked directly at the pilot and said, "Yes, I suppose you would have."

This was only the first of her many records, and it was far from the last time that Amelia Earhart's life would be in danger.

Chapter 4

An Offer She Couldn't Refuse

"Hello," said the voice on the other end of the telephone. "My name is Railey. Captain Hilton Railey."

"Yes?" Amelia couldn't place the name. It was April, 1928. Once again, the Earhart family had moved, this time to Boston. Her sister, Muriel, was a teacher, and Amelia worked in a settlement house, helping poor immigrants adjust to their new lives in America. She wondered why a captain would be calling her.

"You're interested in flying, are you not?" asked Captain Railey. Amelia said she was. That was an understatement. Amelia hadn't been in a plane for four years. To make the move from Los Angeles to Boston, her family had persuaded her to give up flying for a while. She had to trade in her yellow plane for a family car.

Railey went on. "Would you like to do something for the cause of aviation?"

"Such as what?" asked Amelia, suspicious of the strange caller on the other end.

"Such as flying in a plane across the Atlantic."

The caller, a young man in his early thirties, explained that he worked for publisher George Palmer Putnam. Only a year before, Charles Lindbergh—"Lucky Lindy"—had made his historic flight across the ocean. Now, Mr. Putnam thought it was time for a "Lady Lindy."

Amelia was one of several candidates for the flight. After their first meeting, Captain Railey told her, "You will have to go to New York with me to meet the people who would pay the cost of the flight." The all male "jury" that Amelia met in New York agreed with Captain Railey. They had found their "Lady Lindy" after all.

During her interview, the committee explained that Amelia would have a pilot who would be paid $20,000. Amelia would receive no money for her trip, nor for any newspaper articles she might write. It didn't matter. Amelia wanted to be the first woman to cross the Atlantic by air.

Thinking about the dangers of the flight, Amelia wrote what she called "popping off letters." They were to be sent in the event that the plane crashed into the sea. She wrote in one to her father . . .

"Hooray for the last grand adventure! I wish I had won, but it was worthwhile anyway. You know that I have no faith we'll meet anywhere again, but I wish we might. Anyway, goodbye and good luck to you."

She wrote the letter on May 20, 1928 while making final preparations for the flight. By then she had met the two men who would make the trip with her, Bill Stultz and Lou Gordon.

Wilmer L. "Bill" Stultz was a talented man. He was a skilled pilot, navigator, and radio operator. Their mechanic, Lou Gordon, was a twenty-six year old Texan.

The airplane had been named *Friendship*. It was a far cry from the old-fashioned planes Amelia was used to. The big German-built plane had only one set of wings, instead of two. They spanned 72 feet across. The *Friendship's* wings were painted gold, its fuselage bright red-orange. Amelia later explained that the color combination "was not chosen for artistry, but for practical use. If we had come down, orange could have been seen further than any other color."

Their first hop was from Boston to Newfoundland. From there, they took off for Europe. Amelia was the official log-keeper for the flight. She sat crouched near the chart table in the back of the plane, jotting down facts about the flight and her feelings about the experience. It was cold and Amelia was thankful for the fur suit someone had loaned her.

It was difficult for Amelia to keep her log in the darkness of night. That didn't discourage her. She scribbled her thoughts, feeling the edge of the paper with her fingers to write each new line:

"How marvelous is a machine and the mind that made it . . . Bill sits up alone. Every muscle and nerve alert. Many hours to go

. . . I've driven all day and night and know what staying alert means."

After thirteen hours into the flight, Stultz had to rely completely on instruments to fly the plane. The plane was tossed about by winds. Rapid changes in altitude often caused unbearable pressure on the passengers' ears.

In 1928 Amelia was the official log keeper on her first transatlantic flight.

Finally, with just one hour's fuel left, Gordon cried out, "Land! I see land!" Twenty hours and forty minutes had passed since they had left Newfoundland. Now, flying above Burry Port, Wales, the three Americans got their first look at the British coastline.

For Amelia Earhart, life would never be the same. Little did she know what mystery awaited her.

Chapter 5

A Sack of Potatoes

"Ticker tape, receptions, dinners, at least that," Captain Railey smiled as he told Amelia about George Putnam's publicity plans.

"You don't have to tell me what's in store for me," Amelia answered. "I know." She was crossing the Atlantic again, coming home by steamship. Amelia was embarrassed by her sudden fame. "All I contributed to the *Friendship* flight—apart from the fact that accidentally I happen to be the first woman to fly across, or rather *to be flown across*, the North Atlantic—was to lie on the floor of the fuselage like a sack of potatoes and admire the lovely clouds we were flying over. That's all I did, Hilton."

Amelia was instantly famous after flying the Atlantic.

It was a feeling that would bother Amelia for the next four years. No matter how many celebrations, parades, and dinners were held in her honor, she felt she had been that "sack of potatoes." She didn't believe that she deserved the "Lady Lindy" title at all. Only by making the flight across the Atlantic alone, handling the controls herself, would she feel worthy of the honor.

Here Amelia is helped from her plane by George Palmer Putnam,
her husband.

29

Finally, to get away from it all, Amelia took to the air. She would practice long distance flying. In England she had purchased an *Avian,* a small, lightweight two-seater airplane. In a series of flights that eventually would take her 6,000 miles, she flew from New York to Los Angeles and back again. It was the first time a woman had made such a long "air-gypsying" flight.

Amelia is surrounded by a crowd in Oakland, California after completing a transcontinental flight.

Her "gypsy flight" was only the beginning of a number of new "firsts" for Amelia Earhart. When the first Women's Air Derby was announced in 1929, Amelia entered. Some of the male pilots called the race a "powder puff derby." But, to the women flying, this race was serious business. They were out to prove that women were good pilots, even under the strain of a tough contest.

Amelia did not win that day. She and her rival, Ruth Nichols, were neck and neck for the lead as they began the last leg of the eight-day derby trip from Santa Monica, California to Cleveland, Ohio.

Miss Nichols' plane took off first. Suddenly, it dipped its wing and crashed into a tractor parked at the end of the runway. Instead of taking off in turn and automatically winning the derby, Amelia dropped behind to rescue her friend. She finished in third place.

It may have been at the very moment she lost that race that Amelia made her decision. No matter what, she was going back over the Atlantic. This time, she would fly alone.

Chapter 6

Solo Across the Atlantic at Last!

It was 7:13 P. M. on May 20, 1932, five years to the day after Lindbergh soloed to Paris. At this moment, Amelia Earhart began her own historic journey over the Atlantic. She traveled light. The only food she brought was a thermos of hot soup and a can of tomato juice.

From the first minute of flight, everything seemed to go wrong. First, the needle on the altimeter began to spin. Amelia had no way of telling how high she was flying. Then the clouds grew thick. Hard rain drove against the windshield. Lightning bolts surrounded the

After Amelia's solo Atlantic flight in 1932, she caught the attention and admiration of many world leaders. President Hoover presented her with a medal from the National Geographic Society.

plane. More instruments broke down. Amelia dared not take her eyes off the ones that still worked.

Ice began to form on the wings. Suddenly, her plane began to spin out of control. But Amelia's years of flying paid off. She was able to "level it off." Looking out, she realized that she had come dangerously close to the ocean. Should she continue to fly low and hope to melt the ice on the wings? Or should she return to a safer altitude and risk more damage to the instruments?

Amelia decided to climb again, relying only on her instruments for the rest of the trip. She believed in them. She had to. They were more than her "eyes" now. They were her only hope. Fighting fatigue and fear, Amelia soon was aware she had new problems. Fuel had leaked into the cockpit. She now had to fight the stinging odor of gasoline. Her eyes and nostrils burned.

By the time dawn broke, Amelia, tired, stiff, and hungry, was afraid to take her eyes off the instruments or her hands off the throttle. But soon the sun got brighter. She had been flying for ten hours.

On a flight from Washington to Baltimore, Amelia points out places of interest to Mrs. Eleanor Roosevelt.

As Amelia peered out over the horizon, she saw a thin, dark line. Was it more clouds—or was it land? It was too soon to tell. The line grew. It was the coast of Ireland! With the damage to her instruments and little fuel left, Amelia decided that her original destination, Paris, was out of the question. It was time to look for a place to land.

The time was 1:45 P.M., fifteen hours and eighteen minutes after her departure. "Lady

After her world-wide exploits, her home town, Atchison, Kansas, gave Amelia a heroine's welcome when she returned for a visit.

Lindy" didn't have to feel guilty any more. This time she crossed the Atlantic, *by herself.*

But she only had flown across the Atlantic. Someone had done that before she did! Now she would fly the trip no one had ever made. Amelia would have her biggest "first" very soon.

Chapter 7

Last Flight

At five o'clock in the morning, June 1, 1937, Amelia Earhart and her navigator, Fred Noonan, climbed into the *Lockheed Electra* that would take them around the world. There were no weepy goodbyes, no fanfare. Amelia didn't believe in them.

This team—Earhart and Noonan—were going to fly 27,000 miles around the world at the equator. Amelia had always been bothered that what she had done had already been done before—*by men*. Now she was going to do something no man had ever done before, not even "Lindy."

For her planned flight around the world, Amelia decided to carry kites as distress signals to aid searchers in finding her, should she get lost.

The plan was to fly from Miami across the 1,000-mile stretch of the Caribbean to Puerto Rico. The flight would then go on to Brazil, Africa, Karachi, Burma, Singapore, Australia, Howland Island, and Hawaii. Finally, they would fly back to the United States, and land in California.

They traveled 1,000 miles across Africa to India. What would happen if she and Fred came across unfriendly natives in any of these far-off regions? Indeed, at the airfield in El Fasher, they were met by a party of men with guns. The "guns" turned out to be disinfectant sprayers.

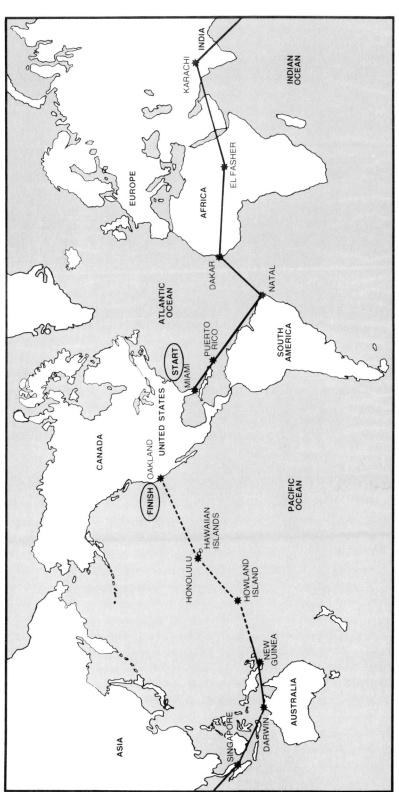

Amelia began her around-the-world flight in Miami, traveling east. She crossed three continents.

Amelia lifts her plane off the runway at Miami on the first leg of her west to east around-the-world flight.

Between India and Australia, the *Electra* ran into the *monsoons*. Amelia had never experienced rain like that before—and the worst was yet to come.

Determined as always, Amelia convinced Fred that they should keep going. They flew through teeming rains and high winds. The plane tossed and pitched. Amelia feared that the force of the downpour would damage the plane.

Somehow, Amelia and Fred made it to New Guinea. Their next stop would be Howland Island, a tiny island in the Pacific, 2,566 miles away. This would be the longest leg of their journey. They had only 7,000 miles to go to complete their round-the-world trip.

On the long trip to Howland, the fliers would have no landmarks to guide them. And once they were more than 500 miles from New Guinea, radio contact would be out of the question. The *Electra* would have to stay on course all night. Then, *if they were directly on target*, an American Coast Guard cutter, the *Itasca*, would talk with them by radio in the morning.

They left New Guinea at 10 A.M. Meanwhile, the crew on the *Itasca* waited for Amelia.

This picture of Amelia and her navigator, Fred Noonan, was taken in New Guinea just before they took off for Howland Island in the Pacific. It is believed to be her last picture.

They had been trying to establish communications with the *Electra* since early that day. Finally, at 2:45 a voice came over the *Itasca's* radio. It was the voice of Amelia Earhart. Her words were difficult to understand because of the heavy static. "Cloudy and overcast" were the only words the crew could make out.

For the next five hours, the *Itasca* tried to reach Amelia again. No contact was made. Then, at 7:42 A.M., Amelia's voice suddenly came in loud and clear. She sounded frantic: "We must be on you," she said. "But cannot see you. Fuel is running low. Been unable to reach you by radio. We are flying at altitude 1,000 feet."

For the next hour, a new struggle for radio contact went on. Amelia's voice was last heard at 8:45 A.M. "We are running north and south" were her parting words.

Though the *Itasca* continued to try to contact the *Electra,* everyone's worst fear soon became an obvious truth—Amelia Earhart and Fred Noonan were lost somewhere in the South Pacific. What had happened to their plane? Had it crashed? *Where was Amelia Earhart?*

Chapter **8**

An Unsolved Mystery

Finally, all hopes of contacting Amelia by radio were abandoned. The world was shocked by Amelia's disappearance. People couldn't understand how she could have vanished. Why could no one find her? The Navy's sixteen-day search of the Pacific had uncovered not a trace of the *Electra*—no wreckage, no bodies. *Where was Amelia?*

The most popular theory at the time was that Amelia and Fred had fallen into the hands of the Japanese. Some people thought the *Electra* had gone off course and illegally crossed over Japanese islands. Japan was at war at that time.

They were suspicious of Americans. The theory was that the Japanese had shot down the plane, thinking that Amelia and Fred were spies.

Five years later, a Hollywood movie helped keep alive the Japanese theory. It was 1942, a year after the Japanese attacked the United States at Pearl Harbor, Hawaii. During that time, Americans saw the Japanese as enemies. The plot of the movie, *Flight for Freedom*, was not supposed to be a true story. The film, however, told a story that was amazingly close to Amelia's last flight. In it, a famous American woman flier, "Tonie Carter," had been asked by the United States Navy to purposely get "lost" in the South Pacific. This secret mission would allow the navy planes to take pictures of Japanese military bases while "looking for Tonie."

Even Amelia's mother believed that her daughter was on a secret mission. She had no evidence to prove it—just a *feeling*. Other people claim to have uncovered actual proof that Amelia was a spy.

A close friend of Amelia's, pilot Jaqueline Cochran, went to Japan shortly after the end of the war. Her mission was to investigate the role of Japanese women in the war. In going through the

Japanese files, Cochran found many records of American aviators, among them several folders on Amelia Earhart. After the war, these files mysteriously disappeared. *Where are they?*

A retired Air Force major, Joseph Gervias, has spent the last twenty years of his life investigating this strange case. He agrees that Amelia was captured by the Japanese while she was on a secret mission for the U.S. But he adds that when Miss Cochran was in Japan, she actually found Amelia. She disguised the famous flier as a nun and secretly returned her to the United States. Gervias, who has studied over 1,000 photographs of the famous flier, believes that Amelia Earhart now lives in New Jersey under a different name. This New Jersey woman, when told about his evidence in 1965, said, "I am not a mystery woman! I am not Amelia Earhart!" *Is this woman Amelia Earhart?* If so, why is she hiding under a different name?

Fred Goerner, another investigator, claims to have learned of secret Japanese papers. He says they prove Amelia was a prisoner on Saipan, a Japanese island 1,500 miles northwest of Howland Island. Visiting the island in 1960 as a news correspondent, Goerner claims to have met several Saipanese people who told him that an

American woman was buried in their cemetery, sometime in 1937. Is this what happened to Amelia Earhart?

Josephine Blanco, a Saipanese woman who now lives in California, supports Goerner's theory. Eleven years old at the time of Amelia's flight, Josephine was taking lunch to her brother-in-law, a soldier living on a quiet part of the island. When Josephine got there, a plane was landing on the water. Everyone was shouting, "The American woman! Come see the American woman!" Josephine remembers being surprised—the American woman with short hair was dressed like a man. Both the woman and the man she was with were pale and sick-looking. Two Japanese soldiers took them into the woods. Shots rang out. Only the soldiers came back.

With all these stories, Amelia Earhart's disappearance is still an unsolved mystery. Was she on a secret mission? Did she have to make a forced landing on a Japanese island because it was the only land in sight? Did the Japanese, sighting an American plane, shoot her plane down? If she were taken prisoner, was she shot immediately? Was she left to die in a prison cell? Is Amelia Earhart still alive and living somewhere in the United States under a different name? Or did her

Amelia was a pioneer in American aviation. Her disappearance
can never erase her contribution to the early history of flight.

plane go down in a remote part of the Pacific where it still lies deeply embedded on the ocean floor?

It has been more than 40 years since the world lost its heroine of the skies. The rumors still fly, the world still remembers Amelia. People won't give up on her. But we really don't have to. Amelia Earhart is a legend—and legends never die. *Neither do unsolved mysteries.*